PENGUIN BOOKS

FELICITY

Born in a small town in Ohio, Mary Oliver published her first book of poetry in 1963 at the age of twenty-eight. Over the course of her long career, she has received numerous awards. Her fourth book, *American Primitive*, won the Pulitzer Prize for Poetry in 1984. She has led workshops and held residences at various colleges and universities, including Bennington College, where she held the Catharine Osgood Foster Chair for Distinguished Teaching. She died in 2019.

# Felicity

*Mary Oliver*

PENGUIN BOOKS

PENGUIN BOOKS

An imprint of Penguin Random House LLC
penguinrandomhouse.com

First published in the United States of America by Penguin Press,
an imprint of Penguin Random House LLC, 2015
Published in Penguin Books 2017

Acknowledgments to the original publishers of several poems appear on page 83.

Excerpts from poems by Rumi, translated by Coleman Barks.
Used by permission of Coleman Barks.

ISBN: 9781594206764 (hardcover)
ISBN 9780143128762 (paperback)

Printed in the United States of America
11th Printing

*Designed by Amanda Dewey*

*For Anne Taylor*

# CONTENTS

## Felicity

# The
# Journey

"You broke the cage and flew."

RUMI

# Don't Worry

Things take the time they take. Don't
   worry.
How many roads did St. Augustine follow
   before he became St. Augustine?

# Walking to Indian River

I'm ready for spring, but it hasn't arrived.
                    Not yet.
Still I take my walk, looking for any
          early enhancements.
*It's mostly attitude.* I'm certain
                    I'll see something.
I start down the path, peering in
          all directions.
The mangroves, as always, are standing in their
                    beloved water,
their new leaves very small and tender
          and pale.
And, look! the way the rising sun
                    strikes them,
they could be flowers
          opening!

# Roses

Everyone now and again wonders about
those questions that have no ready
answers: first cause, God's existence,
what happens when the curtain goes
down and nothing stops it, not kissing,
not going to the mall, not the Super
Bowl.

"Wild roses," I said to them one morning.
"Do you have the answers? And if you do,
would you tell me?"

The roses laughed softly. "Forgive us,"
they said. "But as you can see, we are
just now entirely busy being roses."

# Moments

There are moments that cry out to be fulfilled.
Like, telling someone you love them.
Or giving your money away, all of it.

Your heart is beating, isn't it?
You're not in chains, are you?

There is nothing more pathetic than caution
when headlong might save a life,
even, possibly, your own.

# The World I Live In

I have refused to live
locked in the orderly house of
   reasons and proofs.
The world I live in and believe in
is wider than that. And anyway,
   what's wrong with *Maybe*?

You wouldn't believe what once or
twice I have seen. I'll just
   tell you this:
only if there are angels in your head will you
   ever, possibly, see one.

# Do the Trees Speak?

Do the trees speak back to the wind
when the wind offers some invitational comment?
As some of us do, do they also talk to the sun?
I believe so, and if such belief need rest on
    evidence, let me just say, Sometimes it's
    an earful.

But there's more.

If you can hear the trees in their easy hours
of course you can also hear them later,
    crying out at the sawmill.

# I Am Pleased to Tell You

Mr. Death, I am pleased to tell you, there
are rifts in your long black coat. Today
Rumi (obit. 1273) came visiting, and not for
the first time. True he didn't speak with
his tongue but from memory, and whether
he was short or tall I still don't know.
But he was as real as the tree I was
under. Just because something's physical
doesn't mean it's the greatest. He
offered a poem or two, then sauntered on.
I sat awhile feeling content and feeling
contentment in the tree also. Isn't
everything in the world shared? And one
of the poems contained a tree, so of
course the tree felt included. That's
Rumi, who has no trouble slipping out of
your long black coat, oh Mr. Death.

# Leaves and Blossoms Along the Way

If you're John Muir you want trees to
live among. If you're Emily, a garden
will do.
Try to find the right place for yourself.
If you can't find it, at least dream of it.

.

When one is alone and lonely, the body
gladly lingers in the wind or the rain,
or splashes into the cold river, or
pushes through the ice-crusted snow.

Anything that touches.

.

God, or the gods, are invisible, quite
understandable. But holiness is visible,
entirely.

.

Some words will never leave God's mouth,
no matter how hard you listen.

In all the works of Beethoven, you will
not find a single lie.

.

All important ideas must include the trees,
the mountains, and the rivers.

.

To understand many things you must reach out
of your own condition.

.

For how many years did I wander slowly
through the forest. What wonder and
glory I would have missed had I ever been
in a hurry!

.

Beauty can both shout and whisper, and still
it explains nothing.

.

The point is, you're you, and that's for keeps.

# I Wake Close to Morning

Why do people keep asking to see
        God's identity papers
when the darkness opening into morning
        is more than enough?
Certainly any god might turn away in disgust.
Think of Sheba approaching
        the kingdom of Solomon.
Do you think she had to ask,
        "Is this the place?"

# Meadowlark

Has anyone seen meadowlark?
I've been looking for probably
forty years now

unsuccessfully.

He used to live in the field
I crossed many a morning
heading to the woods,
truant again from school.

There were no meadowlarks in the school.
Which was a good enough reason for me
not to want to be there.

But now it's more serious.
There is no field, neither have the woods survived.

So, where is meadowlark?

If anyone has seen him, please would you let me know posthaste?

# The Wildest Storm

Yesterday the wildest storm
I ever witnessed flew past
west to east, a shaggy
howling sky-beast

flinging hail even as lightning
printed out its sizzling
unreadable language
followed by truly terrible laughter.

But, no. Maybe it wasn't laughter
but a reminder we need—
seemingly something to do with power.

What could it be? What could it be?
What do you think it could be?

# Cobb Creek

It's morning at the creek-edge
   and the question is:
Shall I jump as usual and enjoy,
   as I have hundreds of times,
the casual down-thrust of my legs
   on the other side?

Certain facts are unavoidable, still
   something in me
refuses to abdicate.

I don't spend much time on it.
   I jump
and for the first time in my seventy-seven years
   I fall in.

What a beautiful splash!

# Nothing Is Too Small Not to Be Wondered About

The cricket doesn't wonder
    if there's a heaven
or, if there is, if there's room for him.

It's fall. Romance is over. Still, he sings.
If he can, he enters a house
    through the tiniest crack under the door.
Then the house grows colder.

He sings slower and slower.
    Then, nothing.

This must mean something, I don't know what.
    But certainly it doesn't mean
he hasn't been an excellent cricket
    all his life.

# Whistling Swans

Do you bow your head when you pray or do you look
    up into that blue space?
Take your choice, prayers fly from all directions.
And don't worry about what language you use,
God no doubt understands them all.
Even when the swans are flying north and making
such a ruckus of noise, God is surely listening
    and understanding.
Rumi said, There is no proof of the soul.
But isn't the return of spring and how it
springs up in our hearts a pretty good hint?
Yes, I know, God's silence never breaks, but is
    that really a problem?
There are thousands of voices, after all.
And furthermore, don't you imagine (I just suggest it)
that the swans know about as much as we do about
    the whole business?
So listen to them and watch them, singing as they fly.
Take from it what you can.

# Storage

When I moved from one house to another
there were many things I had no room
for. What does one do? I rented a storage
space. And filled it. Years passed.
Occasionally I went there and looked in,
but nothing happened, not a single
twinge of the heart.
As I grew older the things I cared
about grew fewer, but were more
important. So one day I undid the lock
and called the trash man. He took
everything.
I felt like the little donkey when
his burden is finally lifted. Things!
Burn them, burn them! Make a beautiful
fire! More room in your heart for love,
for the trees! For the birds who own
nothing—the reason they can fly.

# Humility

Poems arrive ready to begin.
　　Poets are only the transportation.

# For Tom Shaw S.S.J.E. (1945–2014)

Where has this cold come from?
"It comes from the death of your friend."

Will I always, from now on, be this cold?
"No, it will diminish. But always
        it will be with you."

What is the reason for it?
"Wasn't your friendship always as beautiful
    as a flame?"

## That Tall Distance

That tall distance where
the clouds begin,
the forge that pounds out the lightning
and the black porch where the stars
are dressed in light
and arrangement is made for the moon's path—
it's these I think of now, after

a lifetime of goldfinches,
meandering streams,
lambs playing,
the passionate hands of the sun,
the coolness under the trees
talking leaf to leaf,
the foxes and the otters sliding on the snow,
the dolphins for whom no doubt
the seas were created,
the spray of swallows gathering in autumn—
after all of that
the tall distance is what I think of now.

# This Morning

This morning the redbirds' eggs
have hatched and already the chicks
are chirping for food. They don't
know where it's coming from, they
just keep shouting, "More! More!"
As to anything else, they haven't
had a single thought. Their eyes
haven't yet opened, they know nothing
about the sky that's waiting. Or
the thousands, the millions of trees.
They don't even know they have wings.

And just like that, like a simple
neighborhood event, a miracle is
taking place.

# Love

"Someone who does not run

toward the allure of love

walks a road where nothing lives."

RUMI

# When Did It Happen?

When did it happen?
  "It was a long time ago."

Where did it happen?
  "It was far away."

No, tell. Where did it happen?
  "In my heart."

What is your heart doing now?
  "Remembering. Remembering!"

# The First Day

After you left
I jumped up and down,
I clapped my hands,
I stared into space.

In those days I was starving for happiness.
So, say it was both silly and serious.
Say it was the first warm sting of possibility.
Say I sensed the spreading warmth of joy.

# I Know Someone

I know someone who kisses the way
a flower opens, but more rapidly.
Flowers are sweet. They have
short, beatific lives. They offer
much pleasure. There is
nothing in the world that can be said
against them.
Sad, isn't it, that all they can kiss
is the air.

Yes, yes! We are the lucky ones.

# No, I'd Never Been to This Country

No, I'd never been to this country
before. No, I didn't know where the roads
would lead me. No, I didn't intend to
turn back.

## I Did Think, Let's Go About
## This Slowly

I did think, let's go about this slowly.
This is important. This should take
some really deep thought. We should take
small thoughtful steps.

But, bless us, we didn't.

# This and That

In this early dancing of a new day—
dogs leaping on the beach,
dolphins leaping not far from shore—
someone is bending over me,
is kissing me slowly.

# How Do I Love You?

How do I love you?
Oh, this way and that way.
Oh, happily. Perhaps
I may elaborate by

demonstration? Like
this, and
like this and

     no more words now

# That Little Beast

That pretty little beast, a poem,
    has a mind of its own.
Sometimes I want it to crave apples
    but it wants red meat.
Sometimes I want to walk peacefully
    on the shore
and it wants to take off all its clothes
    and dive in.

Sometimes I want to use small words
    and make them important
and it starts shouting the dictionary,
    the opportunities.

Sometimes I want to sum up and give thanks,
    putting things in order
and it starts dancing around the room
    on its four furry legs, laughing
    and calling me outrageous.

But sometimes, when I'm thinking about you,
    and no doubt smiling,
it sits down quietly, one paw under its chin,
    and just listens.

# What This Is Not

This is not just surprise and pleasure.
This is not just beauty sometimes
     too hot to touch.
This is not a blessing with a beginning
     and an end.
This is not just a wild summer.
This is not conditional.

# Everything That Was Broken

Everything that was broken has
forgotten its brokenness. I live
now in a sky-house, through every
window the sun. Also your presence.
Our touching, our stories. Earthy
and holy both. How can this be, but
it is. Every day has something in
it whose name is Forever.

# Except for the Body

Except for the body
of someone you love,
including all its expressions
in privacy and in public,

trees, I think,
are the most beautiful
forms on the earth.

Though, admittedly,
if this were a contest,
the trees would come in
an extremely distant second.

# Not Anyone Who Says

Not anyone who says, "I'm going to be
    careful and smart in matters of love,"
who says, "I'm going to choose slowly,"
but only those lovers who didn't choose at all
but were, as it were, chosen
by something invisible
and powerful and uncontrollable
and beautiful and possibly even
unsuitable—
only those know what I'm talking about
in this talking about love.

# The Pond

August of another summer, and once again
I am drinking the sun
and the lilies again are spread across the water.
I know now what they want is to touch each other.
I have not been here for many years
during which time I kept living my life.
Like the heron, who can only croak, who wishes he
    could sing,
I wish I could sing.
A little thanks from every throat would be appropriate.
This is how it has been, and this is how it is:
All my life I have been able to feel happiness,
except whatever was not happiness,
which I also remember.
Each of us wears a shadow.
But just now it is summer again
and I am watching the lilies bow to each other,
then slide on the wind and the tug of desire,

close, close to one another.

Soon now, I'll turn and start for home.

And who knows, maybe I'll be singing.

# Late Spring

Finally the world is beginning
to change, its fevers mounting,
its leaves unfolding.

And the mockingbirds find
ample reason and breath to fashion
new songs. They do. You can
count on it.

As for lovers, they are discovering
new ways to love. Listen, their windows are open.
You can hear them laughing.

Without spring who knows what would happen.
A lot of nothing, I suppose.
The leaves are all in motion now
the way a young boy rows and rows

in his wooden boat, just to get anywhere.
Late, late, but now lovely and lovelier.
And the two of us, together—a part of it.

# A House, or a Million Dollars

People do it,
some out of desperation,
others out of greed.

They steal.

The very powerful and clever
might steal a whole house,
or a million dollars.
It's been done.

But what does it matter?
Love is the one thing the heart craves
and love is the one thing
you can't steal.

# I Don't Want to Lose

I don't want to lose a single thread
from the intricate brocade of this happiness.
I want to remember everything.
Which is why I'm lying awake, sleepy
but not sleepy enough to give it up.
Just now, a moment from years ago:
the early morning light, the deft, sweet
gesture of your hand
    reaching for me.

# I Have Just Said

I have just said
    something
ridiculous to you
    and in response,

your glorious laughter.
    These are the days
the sun
    is swimming back

to the east
    and the light on the water
gleams
    as never, it seems, before.

I can't remember
    every spring,
I can't remember
    everything—

so many years!
   Are the morning kisses
the sweetest
   or the evenings

or the inbetweens?
   All I know
is that "thank you" should appear
   somewhere.

So, just in case
   I can't find
the perfect place—
   "Thank you, thank you."

# The Gift

Be still, my soul, and steadfast.
Earth and heaven both are still watching
though time is draining from the clock
and your walk, that was confident and quick,
has become slow.

So, be slow if you must, but let
the heart still play its true part.
Love still as once you loved, deeply
and without patience. Let God and the world
know you are grateful.
That the gift has been given.

# Felicity

"Out beyond ideas of wrongdoing and rightdoing

there is a field. I'll meet you there."

RUMI

# A Voice from I Don't Know Where

It seems you love this world very much.
　　"Yes," I said. "This beautiful world."

And you don't mind the mind, that keeps you
　　busy all the time with its dark and bright wonderings?
　　"No, I'm quite used to it. Busy, busy,
　　all the time."

And you don't mind living with those questions,
　　I mean the hard ones, that no one can answer?
　　"Actually, they're the most interesting."

And you have a person in your life whose hand
　　you like to hold?
　　"Yes, I do."

It must surely, then, be very happy down there
　　in your heart.
　　"Yes," I said. "It is."

ACKNOWLEDGMENTS

My thanks to the editors of the following magazines, in which some of the poems have previously appeared, sometimes in slightly altered form.

*Appalachia*: "Roses," "Cobb Creek" (under the previous title, "Splash").

*Parabola*: "I Am Pleased to Tell You," "Don't Worry," "Walking to Indian River," "Do the Trees Speak?"

# NOTE

The three quotations from the poet Rumi
are translations by Coleman Barks.

# ALSO AVAILABLE